National
Museums
Scotland

Bonnie
Prince Charlie
and the Jacobites

A SOUVENIR GUIDE

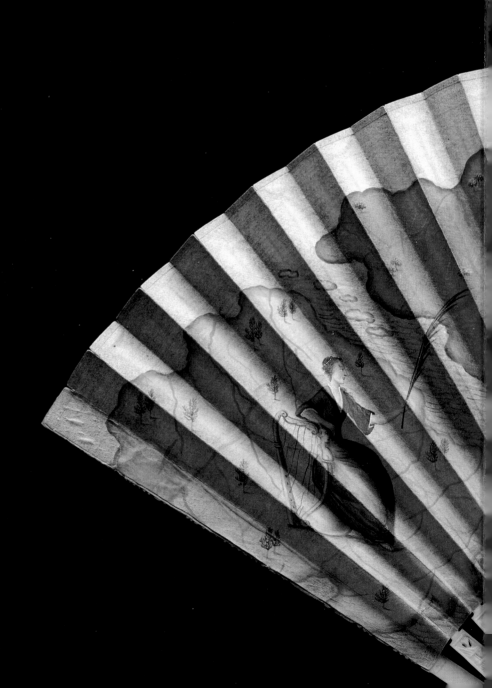

Bonnie Prince Charlie
and the Jacobites

A SOUVENIR GUIDE

Bonnie Prince Charlie and the Jacobites

Exhibition at
National Museum of Scotland
Chambers Street
Edinburgh EH1 1JF

www.nms.ac.uk

23 June to 12 November 2017

Exhibition kindly sponsored by
Baillie Gifford Investment Managers

Book published in 2017 by
NMS Enterprises Limited – Publishing
a division of NMS Enterprises Limited
National Museums Scotland
Chambers Street
Edinburgh EH1 1JF

www.nms.ac.uk

**British Library Cataloguing in Publication
Data**
A catalogue record of this book is available
from the British Library.

ISBN 978 1 910682 09 8

Typesetting by NMS Enterprises Limited –
Publishing.
Cover and design by Mark Blackadder.

Photography (unless otherwise credited) by
NMS Photography.
Printed and bound in Great Britain by
Claro Print, Glasgow.
Cover: Dress targe with silver mounts,
1739–41, part of the accoutrements
presented to Prince Charles Edward
Stuart by James, 3rd Duke of Perth,
National Museums Scotland, H.LN 49.
Pages 2–3: Fan with illustration of Prince
Charles Edward Stuart, mid-18th
century, National Museums Scotland,
H.1994.1052.

Note on date conventions:

Britain and Ireland remained on the Julian
Calendar until the Calendar Act of 1751.
This meant that the British Isles were ten
days behind the Continent in the 17th
century, and eleven days behind for most
of the 18th century. The majority of the
dates in this volume are based on the
Julian Calendar.

For a full listing of NMS Enterprises Limited
– Publishing titles, and related merchandise,
go to:
www.nms.ac.uk/books

Contents

Bonnie Prince Charlie and the Jacobites 7

The Stuart dynasty: Monarchy, faith, power 8

Dynasty restored 10

Dynasty divided 14

A court in exile 20

The challenges of James VIII & III 24

All roads lead to Rome 33

The Jacobite challenge of Bonnie Prince Charlie 41

Kings over the water 60

Death of the king 66

Symbols of support 69

Royal relations 72

Acknowledgements 75

The Stuart dynasty: family tree 76–77

Bonnie Prince Charlie and the Jacobites

In 1745 a young man landed on Eriskay, an island in the Outer Hebrides of Scotland. He had told his father, 'I go sire in search of three crowns … to have the honour and happiness of laying at your majesty's feet'. His father was the exiled Jacobite king James III of England and Ireland, and VIII of Scotland.

The young man was Charles Edward Louis John Casimir Sylvester Maria Stuart, born in Rome on 31 December 1720. Better known as Bonnie Prince Charlie, he was the Jacobites' last hope in the struggle to reinstate a Stuart king to the throne of the three kingdoms. What were the circumstances that compelled him to undertake such a challenge? The answers lie in events that took place almost sixty years earlier.

When the grandfather of Charles – James VII & II – was exiled in 1688, his supporters became known as Jacobites – from '*Jacobus*', Latin for James. Their cause was to restore the exiled Stuart king to the throne of the three kingdoms. When James died, they transferred their allegiance to his heirs.

The Jacobite story – one of exile, war, loss and retribution – spanned three centuries. Conducted in the courts of Europe and fought for on the battlefields of the three kingdoms, it concluded with the burial of three Jacobite kings in St Peter's Basilica, Rome.

Jacobite history is complex. At its core lies one dynasty, the House of Stuart, which was divided into two courts by religion, politics and war. At stake was the throne of three kingdoms – Scotland, England and Ireland. Defeated and forced into exile, four Jacobite kings became part of the wider political games played out in Europe. Despite mounting five challenges they never reclaimed their crown, nor did they fade into obscurity. Their belief and determination ensured their place in history.

The Stuart dynasty
Monarchy, faith, power

Prince Charles Edward came from one of the oldest dynasties in Europe, the Stuarts, who had ruled Scotland since 1371. His great-great-grandfather was James VI of Scotland.

James VI was an infant when he became king in 1567 after the forced abdication of his mother Mary, Queen of Scots. Mary fled to England in the hope of gaining support from her cousin, Elizabeth I. Instead she was imprisoned for 19 years before being executed for treason. Although Elizabeth signed Mary's death warrant, James VI showed little animosity towards the queen, having been estranged from his mother for most of his life. He trod a careful path, not wishing to forfeit his chance to gain the English throne.

Elizabeth was the last Tudor monarch. She died childless in 1603, failing to name her successor. As her closest relative, Mary's son James VI inherited her crown and the kingdoms of England and Ireland.

The Stuarts had done what no other dynasty had managed to do – uniting the three kingdoms of Scotland, England and Ireland under one monarch, James VI & I.

Coronation ampulla of Charles I

The Latin inscription on this unique little phial states that it held the sacred anointing oil used during the coronation of Charles I at Holyroodhouse on 18 June 1633.

Possibly by James Denniestoun, c.1633, Scottish, gold, 12.5 cm (height), National Museums Scotland, H.KJ 164

The Stuart monarchy was driven by faith and power. Like many European monarchies of the time, the Stuarts also believed that their right to rule came directly from God and they were answerable to God alone: a principle of divine right monarchy that emerged during the medieval period.

The Protestant Reformation of the 16th century had divided Europe. While France and Spain remained Catholic – as did Ireland – Scotland, England and Wales adopted the Protestant faith. As the balance of religious faith and political power shifted, many now questioned the principle of rule by divine right. When James VI & I ascended the throne of the three kingdoms, the power of the monarchy was challenged by parliament and religious radicals in both Scotland and England.

Despite power struggles with church and state, James VI & I left a stable monarchy for his son, Charles I. As an Anglican and even more committed to rule by divine right than his father, Charles refused to relinquish any of his power to parliament. Instead he dissolved the parliament in England and waged war in Scotland when the largely Protestant population refused to accept his religious policies.

The Parliamentarians, or Roundheads, fought and defeated the king's Royalist supporters during the Civil Wars. Charles I was arrested, put on trial at Westminster Hall, and on 30 January 1649 executed for treason. The Stuart monarchy had been overthrown by radical faith and parliamentary power.

Left: Communion bread plate

One of two plates from Trinity College Church, Edinburgh. The minister, Thomas Sydserf, was a staunch follower of Charles I and the king's church policies.

By Thomas Kirkwood, *c.*1632–33, Scottish, silver, 50.7 cm (diameter), National Museums Scotland, K.2001.466.5

Right: Harquebusier's helmet

Harquebusiers were armoured cavalrymen. The maker of this helmet produced armour for James VII & II.

By Richard Holden, *c.*1660–68, English, composite steel, The Royal Collection / HM Queen Elizabeth II 2017, RCIN 28137

Dynasty restored

Oliver Cromwell ruled as Lord Protector of the Commonwealth of England, Scotland and Ireland from 1653 until 1658. Cromwell's successor, his son Richard, resigned after less than a year in office, creating an opportunity for a restoration of the monarchy. Although not opposed to the idea, the English parliament was reluctant to relinquish any recently gained power. In Scotland, however, many sought an end to the enforced Cromwellian Union and welcomed the restoration of the Stuart monarchy.

Parliament dictated the conditions for the return of Charles II, who was living in exile, which included pardons for those who opposed the monarchy during the Civil Wars.

Once established on the throne in 1660, Charles bestowed the Scottish title of Duke of Albany on his younger brother James, Duke of York, and made him Lord High Admiral of England. That same year James married Anne Hyde, who had no title. The couple went on to have eight children, although only the princesses Mary (b.1662) and Anne (b.1665) survived into adulthood.

Anne Hyde converted to Catholicism early in her marriage, with James later following suit. Despite this, Charles II insisted that both of his nieces were raised as Protestants, and in 1677 the king arranged a marriage between Princess Mary and her cousin, the Protestant William of Orange. The couple left England soon after their wedding for William's court in the Netherlands.

During the reign of Charles II, anti-Catholic sentiment ran high in both England and Scotland. When the Test Act was introduced in 1673 to exclude Catholics from public office, James resigned as Lord High Admiral rather than deny his faith. This made his conversion to Catholicism public knowledge. And after the death of his wife Anne Hyde in 1671, James's second marriage two years later to the Catholic princess Mary of Modena only added to public distrust.

Opposite: James VII & II (1633–1701), when Duke of York

Charles II's younger brother James, Duke of York, served in the French and Spanish armies during his exile. After the restoration of the monarchy in 1660, James became Lord High Admiral of England.

By Sir Peter Lely (1618–80), c.1665, oil on canvas, 126.1 x 102.1 cm, The Royal Collection / HM Queen Elizabeth II 2017, RCIN 403224

Claims of a Catholic plot to assassinate Charles II and install James as king began to circulate in 1678. Known as the Popish Plot, it proved to be a hoax, but the rumours served their purpose to discredit the king's younger brother and increase anti-Catholic feeling.

It led to attempts in the English parliament to exclude James from ascending the throne in the event of Charles dying without an heir. The Exclusion Crisis ran from 1679 until 1681, during which time three bills were introduced to parliament by the emerging Whig party, calling for James to be excluded on the grounds of his Catholic faith. His own supporters in parliament, later known as Tories, defended his monarchical rights and the bills were ultimately defeated.

During this period James was sent twice to Edinburgh to prevent him from becoming the focus of Protestant anger. Appointed Lord High Commissioner of Scotland, he was the first Stuart to hold court at the Palace of Holyroodhouse since his father Charles I in 1633.

When Charles II died in 1685 without an heir, his brother became King James VII & II of Scotland, England and Ireland. Although at first he was well received as monarch, this soon changed. Later that year the Duke of Monmouth, illegitimate son of Charles II, attempted to seize power. James suppressed the rebellion and had Monmouth executed.

James increased the standing (permanent) army and Catholics were placed in public office in defiance of the Test Act. He also introduced Declarations of Indulgence into Scotland and England in 1687, granting tolerance to all faiths. Such actions were perceived by enemies of the king as an attempt to increase Catholic power and return to absolute monarchy. In May 1688 seven English bishops refused to read the Declaration of Indulgence in church, claiming that the king had exceeded his powers. James had the bishops arrested, although they were later acquitted.

Tensions grew with the imminent birth of a child to James and Mary. Though Mary had nine children, none survived infancy and the largely Protestant population was confident that the next in line to the throne would be James's eldest daughter, Princess Mary, who would restore a Protestant monarchy. On 10 June 1688 Mary of Modena gave birth to a male Catholic heir, Prince James Francis Edward. With the existence of a half-brother, Princess Mary was no longer the immediate successor and the likelihood of a continued Catholic monarchy significantly increased.

Rumours discrediting the legitimacy of the birth began to circulate. Some claimed that the baby was stillborn and a healthy male child had been smuggled into the bedchamber in a warming-pan.

As tensions grew, Princess Mary's husband, William of Orange, was secretly invited to invade England to challenge his father-in-law and ensure his wife's place in the succession.

Opposite: Holyrood altar plate

In 1687 the chapel royal was created by James VII & II for Catholic worship in the Palace of Holyroodhouse. Fellow Catholic, the Earl of Perth, had a full suite of silver altar plate made in London and sent up via Leith to Holyrood in December 1686. Later a locally made Sanctus bell and incense spoon were added.

Chalice, c.1686, 28.5 cm; ciborium and cover, c.1686, 25.5 cm; Sanctus bell, c.1686–87, 12 cm (all height measurements). Lent by the Scottish Roman Catholic Hierarchy.

Incense spoon, c.1686–87, 10.2 cm (length). Lent by the Congregation of the Ursulines of Jesus.

National Museums Scotland, IL.2009.16.1 and 2, 16.3.1 and 2, 16.4, 17.4

Dynasty divided

In November 1688, William of Orange landed 14,000 troops in the south-west of England. He had been assured of little opposition as many of James's supporters had switched allegiance. The only resistance encountered was a small force of Irish Catholic soldiers gathered at Reading, who proved no match for William's men, and the invasion force continued on towards London.

When anti-Catholic rioting broke out in December, James sent his wife and son to safety in France. Attempting to follow them, he was captured and returned to the capital. He succeeded at the second attempt and was finally reunited with his family.

When James fled, the English parliament declared that the king had abdicated and offered Princess Mary her father's crown. She accepted on condition that she would rule jointly with her husband. On 13 February 1689 the couple ascended the English throne as William III and Mary II.

Most of Ireland continued to recognise James as their king, but the Scottish parliament requested submissions from both James and William before making a decision. While William's reply was reasonable, the response from James was hastily scrawled and full of vague threats and promises. It did little to encourage support and the decision was made that he had forfeited his right to rule in Scotland.

On 11 May 1689 William and Mary accepted the Scottish crown. The people of the three kingdoms were now divided into two opposing camps – Williamites and Jacobites.

Determined to reclaim the throne, James had left France for Ireland in March 1689, accompanied by 5000 French troops. Confident of support from his Irish Catholic subjects, he very quickly established control in the country, swelling his army with local recruits. Only Ulster in the north, which had been settled by Scottish and English Protestants, held out against him.

Opposite: James VII & II (1633–1701) [detail]

While in exile in France, a small, continental industry of portrait-painting, copies and prints developed around James VII & II and his heirs. Their supporters, the Jacobites, wanted icons to reinforce and renew their loyalty.

Artist unknown, c.1690, oil on canvas, 120.7 x 98.4 cm, National Portrait Gallery, London, NPG 366

The fighting dragged on throughout 1689 with little gain or resolution until, on 14 June 1690, William III landed at Carrickfergus near Belfast to take command of his army. Bolstered by his arrival, he led his troops to victory at the Battle of the Boyne on 1 July. Following this defeat James withdrew almost immediately from Ireland, abandoning his supporters and returning to France. The challenge in Ireland, however, continued until 1691 when the Jacobites were finally defeated at the Battle of Aughrim in Galway.

In Scotland, many of those loyal to James VII & II were angered by the decision of their parliament to support William and Mary. One such individual was John Graham of Claverhouse, Viscount Dundee, a veteran of Scotland's Covenanting Wars. Dundee had been present at the Scottish parliament in 1689 when William was declared king.

Furious at this outcome, Viscount Dundee raised a mainly Highland army to challenge William III. General Hugh Mackay, commander-in-chief of William's Government forces in Scotland, was dispatched north to confront Dundee. Their armies met at Killiecrankie in Perthshire on 27 July 1689. The Jacobites held the high ground which was best suited to their battle tactic of charging downhill towards their enemies at speed – known as the Highland charge. General Mackay's forces were defeated, although Dundee was fatally wounded during the fighting.

Further defeat in May 1690 by the Williamite forces at the Battle of Cromdale, Speyside, followed by the news of James's setback in Ireland, caused the Jacobites to lose hope. By 1691 the first Jacobite challenge in Scotland was over, but the repercussions in the Highlands were set to continue. Many Highland clans stayed loyal to James in exile and a further Jacobite challenge remained a real threat. In an attempt to exert control over the Highlands, William III demanded that the clans should swear an oath of allegiance to him with a deadline of 1 January 1692 set for their compliance. Those who failed to sign by then would be punished.

Left: Ship's bell from HMS *Dartmouth*

The *Dartmouth*, a fifth-rate frigate of the Royal Navy, was sent to subdue the Jacobite supporters in the Western Isles during the 1690 uprisings. On 9 October the ship was wrecked off Eilean Rubha an Ridire at the southern entrance to the Isle of Mull.

National Museums Scotland, H.HXD 174

Right: Miniature of John Graham of Claverhouse, Viscount Dundee (1648–89) [detail]

By David Paton (d.1709), *c*.1670, ink on paper, 10.5 x 8.3 cm, Scottish National Portrait Gallery, Edinburgh, PG 588

Opposite: Mitre cap bearing the cypher of William and Mary flanked by thistles

c.1690, National Museums Scotland, National Museums Scotland, M.1985.128

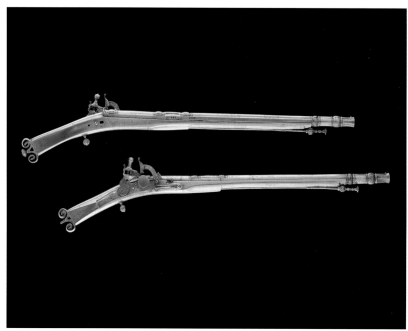

Left: Williamite glass commemorating the Battle of the Boyne, 1 July 1690

*c.*1740–50, English, National Museums Scotland, A.1950.9

Right: Scroll-butt pistols, owned by the Earls of Stair

By Alexander Logan or Adam Lawson, *c.*1660, Scottish, 66 cm (length), National Museums Scotland, H.LH 433 and 434

Opposite: Warrant for a commission of inquiry

This warrant was raised to set up an inquiry into the slaughter of the MacDonalds of Glencoe. The autograph of William III is at the top of the page.

National Museums Scotland, H.OA 37

The MacDonalds of Glencoe failed to make the deadline by a few days. Many of the clans had been waiting to hear from France that they had been released from their oath to James, but the messenger was delayed by atrocious weather. When the MacDonald's chief, MacIain, finally took the oath of allegiance to William, it was declared invalid.

Although MacIain was assured there would be no reprisals, Sir John Dalrymple, 1st Earl of Stair and Secretary of State for Scotland at that time, set out to make an example of the MacDonalds. In February 1692 he sent a unit of the Argyll Militia commanded by Robert Campbell of Glenlyon to be billeted with the clan.

On 13 February, Campbell, who had a personal grudge against the MacDonalds, carried out Dalrymple's order 'to put all to the sword under seventy'. The Massacre of Glencoe saw around 37 members of the MacDonald clan, including its chief, MacIain, murdered.

The Williamite government faced the blame for the massacre and Dalrymple was removed from his post. The atrocity served to increase support in the Highlands for the exiled Jacobite king.

William R

Our Soveraign Lord Considering That Notwithstanding His Ma:ty
did in the year Jaj vj & Ninty three By an express Instruction Impower the deceast William Duke of Hamilton
and others, to take tryall of, and make Inquiry into the Slaughter of the Mcdonalds and others of Glencoe,
in the year Jaj vj & Ninty two, and into the way and manner of Committing it, Yet the Inquiry that was
then made in Prosecution of the foresaid Instruction being defective, And His Ma:ty Considering That
the most effectuall method for getting full Information of the true Circumstances of the said Affair
will be by Appointing an Commission for that Effect. And His Ma:ty being well Satisfied with
the Abilities and Sufficiency of the persons afternamed for the End abovementioned Does therfore
Ordain a Commission to be past and exped under the great Seal of the foresaid Kingdom Nominating
and Appointing Likeas His Ma:ty by these presents Nominats and Appoints His Ma:ts right trusty and right well
beloved Cousins & Counsellors John Marques of Tweeddale Lord High Chancellor of His said Kingdom William Earle of
Annandale His Ma:ts right trusty and well beloved Counsellors John Lord Murray Sir James Stewart His
Ma:ts advocat Adam Cockburn of Ormston His Ma:ts Justice Clerk Sir Archibald Hope of Rankeillor
Sir William Hamilton of Whitelaw Senators of the Colledge of Justice Sir James Ogilvie His Ma:ts solicitor, and Mr Symon of Megginch
wherof five to be a Quorum, and with power to them to chose their own Clerk To be Commissioners
for taking Precognition and making Inquiry into the foresaid Slaughter, by whom, in what manner and
upon what pretended Authority it was committed; And in order to the Discovering of this, The saids
Commissioners are hereby Impowered to call for all the Orders that were given thereanent, As also
to Examine all persons any way concerned therein, And such witnesses as they shall find necessary,
either by taking their Oaths or Declarations And thereafter the said Commissioners are to transmit
to His Ma:ty the true State of the said Affair, together with the Proofs and Evidences which shall
be adduced before them To the effect that after due and full Information, His Ma:ty may give such
necessary Orders thereupon as He shall think propper And His Ma:ty Ordains the foresaid Commission
to be further extended in the most ample forme With all Clauses needfull And to pass his great Seal
aforesaid per Saltum Without passing any other Seal or Register ffor doing wherof these presents
shall be to the Directors of His Ma:ts Chancellary for writing the same And to the Lord High Chancellor
for Causing the Seal be appended therto a Sufficient Warrant Given At His Ma:ts Court at
Kensingtoune the 29 day of Aprile 1695 and of His Ma:ts Reign the 7th year

May it Please your Ma:ty

These contain your Ma:ts Warrant for a Commission to be past under the great Seal of your Kingdom of Scotland
Nominating and Appointing John Marques of Tweeddale your Chancellor And the Lords & others above
named wherof five to be a Quorum To be Commissioners for taking Precognition and making Inquiry
into the Slaughter of the Mcdonalds and others of Glencoe in the year 1692 By whom, in what manner
and upon what pretended Authority It was committed and in order to the Discovery The saids Commis
sioners are Impowered to call for all Orders that were given thereanent and to Examine all persons
that were concerned therein and such witnesses as they shall find necessary, either by taking their oaths or
Declarations And thereafter the said Commissioners are to transmit to y:r Ma:ty the true State of the affair with the
proofs and Evidences which shall be adduced To the End that after due and full Information Your Ma:ty may
give such necessary orders thereon as you shall think propper.

J. Johnstoun

A court in exile

James VII & II and the French king Louis XIV were first cousins and fellow Catholic monarchs. When the safety of his family was threatened, James knew he could count on his cousin's support.

Louis made the château de Saint-Germain-en-Laye available to James and Mary of Modena. Close to Paris and Versailles, it was situated on a plateau high above the river Seine, with a spectacular view towards the city. The château, which had been Louis's main residence before he moved his court to Versailles in 1682, had renowned gardens, a forest ideal for hunting, and a town nearby which provided plenty of extra accommodation for the Jacobite entourage.

The château was lavishly furnished from the royal storehouses and the French king granted James a generous annual pension which enabled him to maintain a large and impressive court of about a thousand individuals. Most of the courtiers were English, although there were also Scots, Irish, French and Italians.

Although smaller than the court they had left behind at the Palace of Whitehall in London, it was impressive nonetheless. The most important members included the gentlemen and ladies of the bedchambers, and the officials in charge of the household departments – the chamber, 'below stairs', and the stables. The governor of the young James Francis, Prince of Wales, was James Drummond, 4th Earl of Perth, and most of the political secretariat were Scottish. These included the Earl of Perth's brother John Drummond (Earl of Melfort). Both he and the Earl of Middleton were secretaries of state; the under-secretary was David Nairne from Fife.

In 1692 Queen Mary gave birth to a daughter, Louise Marie, named after Louis XIV who agreed to be her godfather. The children were brought up as devout Catholics, but also to uphold religious tolerance. Each day the family attended Mass in the chapel royal, with music provided by Italian and French singers and instrumentalists.

As James Francis and Louise Marie grew up, the queen organised balls and concerts for them within the château. There was a stream of visitors to entertain and hunting trips to organise.

The Stuart family regularly visited Versailles, attending official receptions and entertainments that included plays and ballets; while the French king often accompanied them on their hunting trips.

As the years passed, James became resigned to the fact that he would never be restored and his supporters transferred their hopes to his son, James Francis. In order to maintain the profile of the royal children during their exile, the king and queen commissioned portraits and engravings of James Francis and Louise Marie which were sent to loyal Jacobite supporters in the three kingdoms and across Europe.

Louis XIV was determined to secure his cousin's restoration, although his reasons were political and had little to do with family loyalty. When

The Return of James [VIII &] III from Hunting

James Francis Edward Stuart appears here with his governors and equerries. The château de Saint-Germain-en-Laye can be seen in the background on the left.

By Jacob Van Schuppen (1670–1751), 1704, oil on canvas, 98 x 131 cm, Prussian Palaces and Gardens Foundation, Berlin-Brandenburg, Wolfgang Pfauder, F0082756

William III became the ruler of the three kingdoms, he already had a powerful alliance with Spain, the Holy Roman Empire and United Provinces (the Netherlands), created to curb France's expansionist policies – a conflict known as the Nine Years' War. Louis thus sought to weaken this grand alliance by diverting William's attention away from Europe.

James too was confident that, with French backing, his return to power was certain. But after several failed attempts he resigned himself to a life of religious piety and austerity. The Jacobites now placed their hopes in the eventual restoration of his son, James Francis.

The Treaty of Ryswick of 1697 brought the Nine Years' War to an end in Europe, but as part of the peace process Louis XIV was obliged to recognise William III as the *de facto* king of the three kingdoms. The French king, however, continued to consider his cousin the *de jure* king (by law), and James Francis as the Prince of Wales.

As he neared the end of his life, King James VII & II advised his son to 'be a good Catholic, fear God, obey the Queen your mother, and, after God, put all your trust in the King of France'. After James's death in 1701, Louis recognised the young prince as James VIII & III, rightful king of Scotland, England and Ireland. He undertook to care for him as though he were his own son – but only if James Francis Edward Stuart remained a Catholic.

James [VII &] II and family [detail]

By Pierre Mignard (1612–95), 1694, oil on canvas, 66.2 x 76.7 cm, The Royal Collection / HM Queen Elizabeth II 2017, RCIN 400966

The challenges of James VIII & III

James VIII & III was just 13 years old in 1701 when he was recognised by his three most powerful allies – Louis XIV of France, Philip V of Spain and Pope Clement XI – as the rightful king of the three kingdoms. When James mounted his challenges for the British throne in 1708, 1715 and 1719, he discovered that support from his allies was dependent on the ever-changing political climate in Europe.

Opposite: Herald's tabard

A herald's tabard which displays the Stuart arms from the reign of Queen Anne prior to the Act of Union of 1707 when these arms were changed.

Early 18th century, Scottish, National Museums Scotland, A.1888.303

The Act of Union

A number of events led up to the first challenge. By 1700 it was clear that measures were required to secure a Protestant succession in Britain. After the death of Mary II in 1694, William III reigned alone until his death in 1702. As the couple had no children, Mary's sister Anne became queen. The Act of Settlement had been passed in 1701 in the English parliament with regard to the succession, naming Sophia of Hanover, granddaughter of James VI & I (who had united the crowns of Scotland and England in 1603), as heir to the English and Irish thrones if Anne should die without an heir.

Not consulted about the Act of Settlement, Scotland drew up its own Act of Security in 1704. While it was agreed that the successor to the Scottish crown should be Protestant, the final choice would be made by the Scottish parliament alone. Wishing to ensure a smooth succession, England introduced the Alien Act in 1705, including trade sanctions against its northern neighbour that would only be lifted if the Act of Security was repealed and Scotland entered into talks aimed at uniting the two parliaments.

Anne, youngest daughter of James VII & II by his first marriage, succeeded to the throne of the three kingdoms in 1702 and worked to unite the two parliaments. Eventually, on 1 May 1707, both administrations were dissolved and a Parliament of the United Kingdom of Great Britain was established at the Palace of Westminster in London.

Pages 26–27: St Andrew, collar and breast badge or star of the Order of the Thistle

Both James VIII & III and Anne used the Order of the Thistle as a means to encourage loyalty.

St Andrew by John James Edington, 1825–26; collar by John Campbell of Lundie, c.1707–8, Scottish, National Museums Scotland, M.1992.1 and 2; breast badge or star by Thomas Wirgman, c.1820, National Museums Scotland, H.NC 429

Left and middle: Medal

Medal commemorating the Union of the Scottish and English parliaments, 1707. One of the main clauses in the Treaty of Union guaranteed the succession of the Protestant Hanoverians.

1707, silver, 3.5 cm (diameter), National Museums Scotland, H.R 99, obverse and reverse

Right: Medal

Medal marking the failure of the Jacobite invasion of Scotland in 1708. Scottish discontent at the Union prompted the French to send an invasion fleet to Scotland with James on board.

By Martin Smeltzing, 1708, The Netherlands, National Museums Scotland, H.1949.1096

Support for the Union had been driven by necessity on both parts. The Scottish parliament had been passing acts that affected trade, the succession and foreign policy in direct conflict with English policies. Scotland, on the other hand, was in need of the financial benefits a union would bring. In the 1690s many Scots had invested in the Darien Scheme, an attempt to establish a Scottish colony in Panama in Central America, with the promise of a lucrative overland trade route. Its failure had driven Scotland to near bankruptcy.

The Union itself was not a simple undertaking, as the two different administrations struggled to merge into one parliament. With many Scots furious about a single parliament governed from London, support for the Jacobite cause grew and conditions were ripe for a challenge.

The Jacobite challenge of 1708

The 1708 campaign by James VIII & III was funded by Louis XIV. At war with Britain over the Spanish succession, the French king saw an opportunity to divert British troops. The attempt, however, proved shambolic. James contracted measles and the French invasion fleet had to wait for his recovery, costing them the element of surprise. As they reached the Firth of Forth on the east coast of Scotland, the Royal Navy was lying in wait. James demanded to be set ashore, but this was refused. Under attack, the French fled for home.

The Jacobite challenge of 1715

The 1715 rising was the only challenge to be raised in Britain without support from a foreign invasion force.

When Queen Anne died in 1714 the Act of Settlement came into effect. As Sophia of Hanover predeceased Anne, the crown passed to Sophia's son George. By the terms of the Union, Scotland agreed to the Hanoverian succession, but when the Union itself failed to deliver economic benefits, resentment grew and many Scots looked to a Jacobite restoration. Support in the north of England was also evident, although many English Jacobites had already been imprisoned at the threat of a possible rising.

The Earl of Mar, a staunch supporter of the government, had been snubbed by George I. Leaving London for Scotland, Mar switched allegiance and raised an army of over 15,000 men in the name of James VIII & III.

On 13 November 1715 Jacobite and Hanoverian forces faced each other at the Battle of Sheriffmuir in Perthshire. Although the Jacobites outnumbered the Hanoverian forces under the Duke of Argyll, Mar did not press their advantage and there was no clear winner. At the same time, in Lancashire, England, Jacobites were defeated at the Battle of Preston.

The arrival of James at Peterhead in the north-east of Scotland on 22 December 1715 did little to rally support. On 4 February James returned to France accompanied by the Earl of Mar. Poor military leadership had denied the Jacobites success.

Left: Broadsheet showing 'Prince James [VIII & III] landing at Peterhead', 22 December 1715

Paper, 55.9 x 40.6 cm, National Library of Scotland. On long term loan to the Scottish National Portrait Gallery, Edinburgh

Right: Earl of Mar

The 1715 Jacobite rising was led by the Earl of Mar who was known as 'Bobbing John' because he switched sides and was indecisive as a general.

Engraving, National Museums Scotland, M.1950.666

Left: Printed cloth

Pale red silk cloth printed in black, in Latin, showing the Confession of Faith of William MacNair. It is dedicated to King Phillip V of Spain and the inhabitants of Seville.

1715, Spanish, silk, 56 x 83.5 cm, National Museums Scotland, A.1942.43

Right: Goblet

Decorated with horsemen and war trophies, this goblet was made to commemorate the 1718 Quadruple Alliance of France, the Dutch Republic, Austria and Britain. The alliance was a response to Spanish aggression in Italy, although it did not stop Spain under Philip V seizing control of Sardinia and Sicily, angering the allied countries.

*c.*1720, Bohemian, glass, 19.7 cm (height) x 12.1 cm (diameter), National Museums Scotland, A.1979.404

Opposite: *The Battle of Glenshiel* [detail]

By Peter Tillemans (*c.*1684–1734), 1719, oil on canvas, 118 x 164.5 cm, Scottish National Portrait Gallery, Edinburgh, PG 2635

The Jacobite challenge of 1719

Hostilities broke out in 1718 between Spain and the Quadruple Alliance of France, the Dutch Republic, Austria and Britain. As part of this alliance – and as a condition of the Treaty of Utrecht of 1713 (which brought the Spanish War of Succession to an end) – the French were not allowed to offer support to the Jacobites. James VIII & III instead approached Philip V of Spain to seek military help to restore him to the throne of Britain. If successful, Spain would gain a powerful Catholic ally in Europe.

In 1719 Philip sent a small diversionary force to the West Highlands, while a larger fleet headed for the south-west of England. Once the invasion was underway, James, who had been negotiating in Spain, would join them.

Although the smaller force landed as intended, the main fleet was destroyed by a storm. Unaware of events, the Jacobites and Spanish allies established their headquarters at Eilean Donan Castle in the Kyle of Lochalsh and waited.

When news came there would be no further military support from Spain, the Jacobites determined to stand and fight. On 10 June 1719 they were defeated by the Hanoverian forces at the Battle of Glenshiel in the north-west Highlands. The Highland soldiers were encouraged to disband by their commanders, while the captured Spanish troops were marched south to face imprisonment in Edinburgh. They were later released and returned to Spain.

All roads lead to Rome

Early in 1712 James Francis and his sister Louise Marie contracted smallpox. Although James Francis recovered, his beloved sister died.

In 1713 the Treaty of Utrecht forced Louis XIV to end his military support for the exiled Stuarts, but also to have James Francis and his court expelled from France. The French king arranged for James to move from Saint-Germain-en-Laye to Bar-le-Duc in the independent Duchy of Lorraine, and from 1713–15 the Duchy provided him with a base for his court. His mother, Mary of Modena, stayed on at Saint-Germain until she died in May 1718.

With the death of Louis XIV in 1715, James lost his closest ally. Returning from Scotland after the failed rising of 1715, he faced the new regent of France, Philip II, Duke of Orléans. Philip, who was anti-Jacobite, refused to let James back into Lorraine, so James set up court in Avignon, a papal territory within France. In 1717 Philip forced him to leave yet again. This time James moved to Italy, to the Papal States, where he established his court at Urbino, finally settling in Rome in 1718.

While at Urbino thoughts turned to marriage. Charles Wogan, an Irish Jacobite who served James at Avignon, was asked to find a suitable bride and suggested the Polish princess, Maria Clementina Sobieska. She was an excellent match for James – devoutly Catholic, a goddaughter of Pope Clement XI, and she brought with her a substantial dowry.

George I, on hearing of the impending marriage, feared a further threat to the Hanoverian monarchy should the couple have children. He asked the Holy Roman Emperor, Charles VI, to have Maria Clementina arrested as she travelled through Austria en route to her marriage.

As James was already in Spain preparing for the 1719 invasion of Britain, Wogan assisted Maria Clementina's escape from Austria and a proxy marriage was arranged on her arrival in Bologna on 9 May. When James returned to Italy after the failure of the Spanish invasion, he met his

34

bride in person at Montefiascone, just outside Rome, where they solemnised their marriage on 3 September.

Pope Clement XI secured the Palazzo Muti in Rome for the newlyweds. Renamed the Palazzo del Re ('Palace of the King'), this extensive 17th-century building was situated near the Pope's own palace, the Quirinale. Large enough to accommodate almost all the Jacobite courtiers, James now had a permanent court, paid for by the Papal Treasury.

In December 1720 Maria Clementina gave birth to Prince Charles Edward, the future 'Bonnie Prince Charlie'. She had another son in March 1725, Prince Henry Benedict. The marriage, however, was not a happy one. Maria Clementina was a spirited woman with a fierce temper, who did not trust some of her husband's closest confidants. James, believing her to be too young to manage her own household, had Charles taken away from her care at four years of age instead of the customary seven. The young boy was raised by the men of the court including James Murray, a Scottish Protestant. The devoutly Catholic Maria Clementina was enraged and left the Palazzo del Re to take refuge in a convent.

As the Pope took Maria Clementina's side in their dispute, James went with his sons to Bologna from 1726–29 when a compromise was finally reached. Murray, however, remained as Charles's governor, while Maria Clementina became increasingly withdrawn and her health declined. She died in 1735 aged 33 and was buried in St Peter's Basilica in Rome, one of only two queens accorded this honour.

Above: Valances from a set of wall hangings

These valances are a Scottish domestic expression of Jacobite support through a tribute to the marriage of James VIII & III and Maria Clementina. The central sunflower symbolises constancy to a monarch, surrounding the crowned initials of the couple, 'IRCR', and the date of their marriage, 1719.

Possibly by Anne Urquhart of Newhall, 1719, Scottish, wool, linen and silk, National Museums Scotland, A.1988.263 C

Opposite: Miniature portrait of Clementina Sobieska, wife of James Francis Edward Stuart

By Antonio David (1680–1737), 1730, oil on canvas, 74 x 62 cm (unframed). Lent by the Pininski Foundation, Warsaw, Poland.

Left: Miniature of Charles aged two

From a collection of Jacobite relics amassed by the Jacobite supporter Sir John Hynde Cotton and his descendants.

Artist unknown, 1723, oil on copper, 7.3 x 5.4 cm, National Museums Scotland, H.NT 244

Right: Miniature of Charles and Henry

This double miniature is a later copy after the court painter Jean-Étienne Liotard. It closely resembles Liotard's own miniature versions of the two princes made when they were around 15 and 10 years of age.

After Blanchet, c.1735, watercolour on bone, 5.9 x 8.2 x 3.7 cm, National Museums Scotland, H.NT 246

Opposite: Prince Henry Benedict Stuart (1725–1807), later Cardinal York

Henry is wearing the insignia of both the Order of the Garter and Thistle.

By Louis Gabriel Blanchet (1705–72), c.1739, oil on canvas, The Royal Collection / HM Queen Elizabeth II 2017, RCIN 401209

Regardless of his marital difficulties, James was a popular figure in Rome and treated as the *de jure* king of Scotland, England and Ireland. As the papacy refused to recognise the Hanoverian monarchs in London, the Jacobite court became a surrogate embassy for British and Irish 'Grand Tourists' in Rome, offering visitors Anglican services, access to medical assistance and diplomatic protection.

James hoped for a restoration after the death of George I in 1727, but the peaceful succession of George II cast doubt that he himself would ever recover his thrones. Jacobite hopes increasingly turned to Charles and Henry, the young Stuart princes. To maintain their profile as the rightful inheritors of the three kingdoms, James commissioned many portraits of his sons, showing them wearing the English Order of the Garter and the Scottish Order of the Thistle.

As the elder son Charles was prepared for kingship, observing close-hand military operations at the Siege of Gaeta at 13 years of age. Henry, five years younger, was forbidden to go.

Both boys were musical and well educated. In character Charles, like his mother, was prone to bouts of elation and melancholy; Henry was more measured and with the same deeply devout Catholic faith as his parents.

During the reigns of George I and II there was widespread support for the Stuarts in the three kingdoms. Thousands of Catholic Irishmen left their homes to join the Jacobite regiments in the armies of France and Spain. Many Scots also followed James Francis into exile after the rising in 1715,

some joining the court in Rome. These included John and Marjory Hay, who were given the Jacobite titles of Lord and Lady Inverness, and James Murray, who became the Jacobite Lord Dunbar. Though these individuals dominated the smaller court in Rome, they were disliked and distrusted by Maria Clementina.

Jacobite supporters in Scotland included James Drummond, 3rd Duke of Perth, who sent a full set of Highland dress to each of the princes, with traditional Highland weapons. In England many Tories also continued to support the exiled Stuarts. Sir John Hynde Cotton, for example, was a member of parliament who corresponded with James and encouraged the French to launch an invasion of England. A spirit of optimism thus prevailed in the Palazzo del Re that Charles, who turned 21 in 1741, would recover the thrones of his father and grandfather. James, however, was well aware that any invasion of Britain would require French military assistance.

In 1743 France and Britain were once again at war. With hostilities escalating, the French king, Louis XV, agreed to provide military support for a Jacobite invasion as a diversionary tactic. Having been made Prince Regent and authorised to act on his father's behalf, Charles left for France in 1744. But when a storm destroyed the French fleet, Louis abandoned his plans. With no more support forthcoming, Charles took the initiative in July 1745 and left France for Scotland. With only two ships and seven loyal kinsmen, he was relying on his conviction that the Highland clans would rise to support him. The final Jacobite challenge had begun.

Opposite and above left: Travelling canteen belonging to Prince Charles Edward Stuart

This canteen was lost, along with much of the prince's other baggage, at the Battle of Culloden and fell into the hands of the Hanoverian commander, William, Duke of Cumberland. He presented it to his *aide-de-camp* George Kepple, Lord Bury, later Earl of Albemarle, and it remained in Kepple's family until 1963.

By Ebenezer Oliphant, 1740–41, Scottish, silver and silver gilt, 16.5 x 10.5 cm. National Museums Scotland, H.MEQ 1584.1 to 16

Right: Targe belonging to Prince Charles Edward Stuart

The cap badges on the Scots bonnets which form part of the decoration are engraved with the crest, motto and St Andrew badge of James Drummond, 3rd Duke of Perth.

1739–41, wood, pigskin, silver mounts, jaguar skin, 47 cm (diameter), National Museums Scotland, H.LN 49

The Jacobite challenge of Bonnie Prince Charlie

Action between HMS Lion *and* Elizabeth *and the* Du Teillay, 9 July 1745

By Dominic Serres (1722–93), 1780, oil on canvas, 40.6 x 61 cm, National Maritime Museum, BHC0364

Prince Charles Edward Stuart left France for Scotland on 7 July 1745 on board the *Du Teillay*, accompanied by the escort ship *Elizabeth*. On 9 July they were intercepted by HMS *Lion* of the Royal Navy. An intense gun battle ensued which lasted around four hours. Both French ships managed to escape, but HMS *Lion* was badly damaged in the engagement. It was an eventful beginning to the 1745 rising.

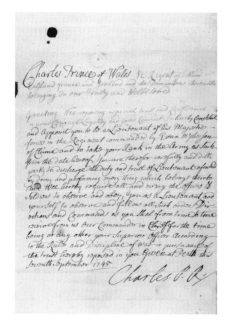 

Left: Commission

Signed by Charles Edward P.R. [Prince Regent], this is one of several commissions entrusted to Ewan Macpherson, who was engaged in raising forces for the prince.

7 September 1745, ink on paper, National Museums Scotland, H.OA 60

Right: Pair of beakers

Engraved with the coat of arms for John Hay, 4th Marquess of Tweeddale, Secretary of State for Scotland during the rising of 1745 and a key Hanoverian supporter.

By James Ker, 1737–38, Scottish, silver, 9.5 x 9 cm, National Museums Scotland, K.2004.207.1 and 2

Opposite: Movement of a pocket watch found near Prestonpans

Recovered from a field near the site of the battle, it was one of the earliest acquisitions by the Society of Antiquaries.

By John Moncrieff, late 17th or early 18th century, English, 4 cm (diameter), National Museums Scotland, H.NL 9

The prince landed on the Isle of Eriskay on 23 July 1745 and set sail for the mainland of Scotland. He faced an uncertain welcome, but when advised to return home he responded, 'Sir I am come home. … I am persuaded that my faithful Highlanders will stand by me'.

Undeterred, Charles managed to win the support of Donald Cameron of Lochiel (the 'Gentle Lochiel'), who encouraged others to join the prince's cause. By 19 August the Stuart standard was raised at Glenfinnan.

Hearing rumours of the prince's presence in the Highlands, a small infantry force was despatched north by the government under the command of Sir John Cope. Both sides failed to engage and the Jacobite army marched swiftly south through Dunkeld to Perth. By 15 September the prince was camped outside Edinburgh ready to begin negotiations for its surrender. With Cope's army advancing, Lochiel and around 900 Highlanders were sent in to take control of the capital. When the gates opened to allow a carriage through, Lochiel's men rushed in, overpowering the city guard. Only the Hanoverian garrison at Edinburgh Castle held out against the Jacobite army.

To the loud cheers of Jacobite supporters, Charles arrived at the Palace of Holyroodhouse and passed under the Stuart armorials to enter the home of his ancestors. At noon the prince had his father, James VIII & III, declared King of Scotland, England and Ireland from Edinburgh's Mercat Cross, a traditional site for important public proclamations. Charles was then announced as Prince Regent.

The Battle of Prestonpans

Sir John Cope sailed from Aberdeen on 15 September intent on halting the Jacobite army before it reached Edinburgh, but he was already too late. Cope landed at Dunbar two days later and led his troops towards the capital.

Alerted to Cope's advance, the prince marched his army east and camped near Prestonpans. On 21 September he led the Jacobites to victory in the first major battle of the campaign. Many of Cope's young and inexperienced soldiers were completely overwhelmed by the speed and ferocity of the Jacobite attack.

The Highlanders used the high ground to best advantage to mount their Highland charge. They ran at Cope's men, firing their muskets, before discarding them to allow free use of their broadswords. Failing to rally his men, Cope made a hasty retreat to Berwick.

In the aftermath of the battle, Charles sent surgeons to attend to all the wounded. He declared that there should be no public rejoicing over the victory. It did not matter on which side a soldier fought, they were all his father's subjects.

Left: Silk gown

This was reputedly worn by Margaret Oliphant of Gask when she attended the court at the Palace of Holyroodhouse.

*c.*1745, British, silk, National Museums Scotland, A.1964.553 and A

Middle and opposite: Tartan frock coat

Short tartan frock coat with velvet collar and cuffs that supposedly belonged to the prince.

Mid-18th century, velvet, wool and twill, National Museums Scotland, K.2002.1031

Right: Sleeved waistcoat

Yellow waistcoat embroidered with a silver floral design, thought to have been worn by the prince.

1727–60, Scottish, silk, National Museums Scotland, A.1906.337

There was little time for ceremony at the newly-established court at the Palace of Holyroodhouse as the days were dominated by official business and campaign planning. Charles was recorded as working diligently, with little if any time to indulge his favourite pastimes, such as dancing, music and hunting. The court was also busy, as curious onlookers flocked to see the young Stuart prince.

Given the major role the clans were set to play in the 1745 rising, there was a need to associate the prince with this key group of supporters, and the wearing of the 'Highland habit' of a clan chief was a highly visible means of connecting with them. When Prince Charles arrived in Edinburgh it was noted that 'he wore the Highland dress … a tartan short coat without the plaid, crimson velvet breeches, and military boots; a blue bonnet … and on his breast the Star of the Order of St Andrew'. Charles had been known to wear Highland dress at recent masquerades and balls in Rome. One account stated that he went 'after ye opera to a publick Ball, masked in a fine complete Highland Dress which became him very well' – possibly the set of Highland clothes and accoutrements sent to him by James Drummond, 3rd Duke of Perth, only six months before the prince sailed for Scotland (see page 39).

The majority of miniatures that circulated around Scotland during this time also show Charles wearing tartan – portrayed as the supreme Highland chief.

RENDER TO CAESAR THE THINGS THAT ARE CAESARS

This page: Silk gown [detail] (see page 44).

Opposite: Fan [detail]

Fan with a hand-painted leaf showing Prince Charles Edward Stuart.

Mid-18th century, National Museums Scotland, H.1994.1052

Left: Portrait of Prince Charles Edward Stuart painted by Allan Ramsay

This portrait of the prince was painted at the Palace of Holyroodhouse at the time a Stuart court was re-established there in autumn 1745. The prince is depicted wearing conventional court dress with the Star of the Order of the Garter.

By Allan Ramsay (1713–84), 1745, oil on canvas, 26.8 x 21.8 cm, Scottish National Portrait Gallery, Edinburgh, PG 3762

Right: Snuff box

Snuff boxes were useful objects to conceal images of the prince. This example has an inner lid which, when opened, reveals a secret enamelled portrait of Charles Edward Stuart. The portrait is based on the work of Allan Ramsay and Robert Strange.

Hardwood, pinchbeck and enamel, 3.2 cm (height), 6.5 cm (diameter), National Museums Scotland, H.NQ 470

It was while the prince held court at Holyroodhouse that the only portrait of him was painted during his time in Britain between 1745 and 1746. In this portrait, by the well-known artist Allan Ramsay, the prince is shown in conventional European court dress and there is no sign of tartan or any other association with Scotland. This is because the portrait was almost certainly aimed at those other than his Scottish followers. Given the prominence of his Order of the Garter star, Charles was being portrayed as a prince of the English realm, in preparation for his march south to take the throne in London.

Charles had occupied Edinburgh for almost six weeks when word reached him that General George Wade and his Hanoverian troops were at Newcastle. On 30 October the prince and his military commanders, including the Duke of Perth, Lord George Murray, Lord Elcho and the Highland chiefs, held a council of war.

Charles was determined to march to Newcastle and engage Wade in battle. Murray and the Highland chiefs proposed they move on Carlisle instead, giving their supporters in England time to join them. On 31 October Charles agreed to Murray's plan. The Jacobite army numbered just under 6000 at this time and included a body of French and Irish troops. Four French ships had arrived with weapons and supplies earlier in the month.

On 8 November the Jacobites crossed the border into England. By 10 November they had reached Carlisle. Five days later the town and castle surrendered. On 4 December the prince's army reached Derby. They were

now within striking distance of the city of London. But despite their progress, cracks were beginning to show in the prince's relationship with some of his commanders, in particular Murray.

Meanwhile Prince William, Duke of Cumberland, the youngest son of George II, had been recalled from the war in Flanders to take command of the Hanoverian forces. Arriving in London on 19 October, he immediately set out with his troops to head off the Jacobites.

At Derby the prince received news that Cumberland's troops were at Lichfield just south of the town. At the same time General Wade was approaching from the north, while soldiers were gathering on Finchley Common to defend London. Charles was determined to continue southwards, even though the anticipated support from English Jacobites and French reinforcements had failed to materialise. His commanders advised moving north again and on Friday 6 December the retreat began.

By late December the Jacobite army reached Glasgow. Then, at the Battle of Falkirk on 17 January, the Hanoverian army led by General Henry Hawley was once again subjected to the Highland charge that had proved so successful at Prestonpans. Yet despite a victory, the Jacobites were still an army in retreat.

The prince and his council of war disagreed over strategy as the Jacobite army moved towards Inverness. By 14 April they were camped at nearby Culloden, with provisions now in short supply. The Duke of Cumberland's forces meanwhile were assembled to the east at Nairn.

A Representation of the March of the Guards towards Scotland in the 1745

An engraving of a William Hogarth satirical painting, it depicts soldiers gathering at Tottenham Court Turnpike north of London before encamping at Finchley Common for the defence of the city.

From a painting by William Hogarth, 18th century, paper, etching, engraving, National Museums Scotland, M.1954.508

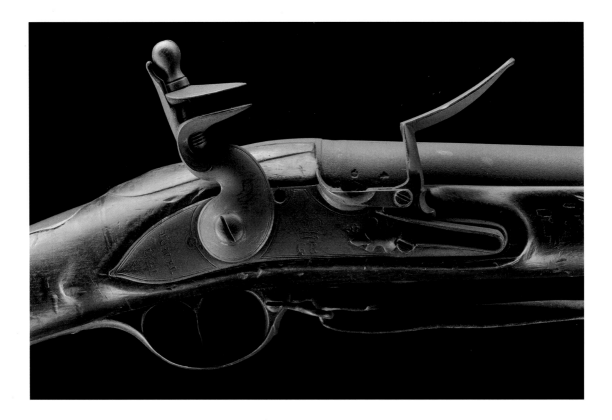

Above: British infantry musket [detail]

Known as a 'Brown Bess', this Long Land pattern musket is said to have been used by a Hanoverian soldier at Culloden.

1742–46, steel, wood and leather, 155.5 cm (length), National Museums Scotland, K.2002.980

Opposite: Portrait of General HRH Prince William Augustus, Duke of Cumberland

Artist unknown, 1746–70, oil on canvas, National Museums Scotland, M.1990.141

Pages 52–53: *An Incident in the Rebellion of 1745* [detail]

Hand-to-hand combat between a party of Highland soldiers and a Grenadier company of the 4th King's Own (Barrel's) Regiment.

Attributed to David Morier (*c.*1705–70), mid-18th century, oil on canvas, 74.6 x 114.6 cm, The Royal Collection / HM Queen Elizabeth II 2017, RCIN 401243

On 15 April a night attack by the Jacobites on Cumberland's forces at Nairn proved disastrous. Tired and hungry, the prince's men became disorientated and the mission had to be abandoned. Making their way back to Culloden, the operation had cost them dearly.

On 16 April both sides met on Drumossie Moor by Culloden. The Jacobite army was made up of Scottish, English, French and Irish troops, while the Hanoverian forces included Scottish regiments. Highlanders fought on both sides.

The prince disregarded advice from Murray and the Highland chiefs that it was neither the right time nor place to do battle. Exhausted and outnumbered, the Jacobite army now faced Cumberland's troops, who were stronger, better-armed and well prepared.

After standing under withering artillery bombardment, the Jacobite regiments advanced across boggy ground into heavy musket fire. The right of the Jacobite army managed to penetrate the opposition's front line, but they were halted and forced back with severe losses. With the Hanoverian cavalry breaking through on the flanks, the Jacobites began to retreat.

Little mercy was shown to the wounded. Fleeing soldiers were chased down and killed along the road to Inverness. Unable to accept the carnage that lay before him, the prince was led from the battlefield in utter shock and disbelief that his army had been defeated.

16 April 1746 The Battle of Culloden

In the immediate aftermath of the battle, the brutality of the Hanoverian army knew no bounds. Cumberland became known as the 'butcher', though his supporters hailed him as a hero for putting down the 'Young Pretender' and his rebellious army.

In the months following the battle his troops occupied and laid waste to areas of Jacobite support, rounding up suspects, burning houses, driving off livestock and dealing out summary justice. Even staunch Hanoverians were shocked by the reports of atrocities.

The reprisals did not last long. Parliament introduced laws that placed the power of retribution into the hands of courts rather than the military. Those who had fought for the Jacobite prince were treated as rebels and traitors – 3472 Jacobites were arrested, 120 sentenced to death, and 900 deported to America and the Caribbean as indentured servants. A list of 240 individuals accused of high treason was published in 1747. Jacobite nobility were beheaded. Commoners were hung, drawn and quartered. Around 1300 prisoners were released without trial, and only a few were pardoned.

The Act of Proscription came into affect on 1 August 1746, designed to end the military culture of Highland clanship based on members bearing arms for their chief in return for tenanted land. Highland chiefs were stripped of their powers of justice and the Disarming Act of 1725 rigorously reinforced as swords, dirks, pistols and targes were seized. The Dress Act banned the wearing of Highland dress, even among those who fought for the Hanoverian army.

In a matter of months, military force and legislation accelerated the economic and social changes that were already dismantling traditional clan society.

Left: Mourning rings

Rings that commemorate the executions of Lord Lovat (above) and the 'Four peers' (below) – Kilmarnock, Derwentwater, Balmerino and Lovat.

National Museums Scotland, H.NJ 88 and H.NJ 154

Right: Pin cushion

There are 67 names printed on this cushion, with the words 'MART:FOR:K:&COU:1746' ['Martyred for King and Country 1746'].

1746, British, satin, 7.5 x 5.7 cm, National Museums Scotland, A.1987.258

Opposite: Print [detail]

This hand-coloured print shows a view of the Battle of Culloden.

Laurie and Whittle (publishers), 1797, hand coloured print, National Museums Scotland, M.1993.250

This page: Gaelic bible [and detail] carried by a Hanoverian soldier at Culloden

Alexander Anderson, who carried this bible, served with the Argyll Militia, a regiment raised by Clan Campbell to fight on the Hanoverian side. This version of scripture is known as Kirk's Bible after the Episcopalian clergyman Robert Kirk who adapted an Irish Gaelic bible for use in Scotland.

18th century, paper and leather, National Museums Scotland, M.L1930.173

Opposite: Medicine chest

Stuart Threipland became a fellow of the Royal College of Physicians in 1744. In 1745 he joined the Jacobite forces and was appointed physician-in-chief to the prince who presented this medicine chest to him.

Mid-18th century, wood, brass, glass. Lent by the Royal College of Physicians of Edinburgh.

And what of the fate of Prince Charles Edward Stuart? Immediately after the battle, the Jacobite soldiers who had managed to retreat safely gathered at Ruthven Barracks awaiting orders from the prince. He eventually sent word thanking them for their bravery and devotion, instructing them to do what was best for their own preservation.

From then, the prince spent five months evading capture in the Highlands and Islands. Not everyone he encountered provided assistance; and those who did were not all Jacobite supporters. Many were imprisoned, exiled or even executed for helping him, yet despite a £30,000 reward Charles was not betrayed.

Flora MacDonald risked her own safety to help the prince, though not an ardent Jacobite. For her part in his escape to the Isle of Skye she was arrested and sent to the Tower of London. On her release she returned home and married Allan MacDonald of Kingsburgh in 1750. They later emigrated to North Carolina in America, where Allan fought for the British during the American War of Independence. Flora died on Skye in 1790.

Other individuals such as Alexander MacDonald of Kingsburgh on the Isle of Skye made his home available to the prince and was arrested for doing so. And Dr Murdoch MacLeod on the island of Raasay also helped Charles to evade capture.

Angus MacDonald of Borrodale, Skye, and his wife Catriona, who had been among the first to welcome the prince when he first arrived in 1745, offered shelter to him on his last night in Scotland in 1746.

Prince Charles Edward and several of his supporters then sailed from Borrodale just before midnight on 19 September on a French ship *L'Heureux,* arriving ten days later at the port of Roscoff in northern France.

Left: Snuff box

This tortoiseshell snuffbox was bequeathed to the Museum by the chief and captain of Clanranald. A treasured clan heirloom, it is engraved with Flora MacDonald's initials 'FMD' on its lid.

18th century, Scottish, silver and tortoiseshell, 6.2 x 3.5 x 1.6 cm, National Museums Scotland, H.MCR 8

Right: Tea caddy

A tea caddy said to have been at Kingsburgh House during the time Prince Charles Edward stayed there. Kingsburgh House was the family home of Flora MacDonald's husband, Allan MacDonald.

18th century, pewter, 9.5 x 10.7 x 7.8 cm, National Museums Scotland, H.MCR 9

Opposite: Portrait of Flora MacDonald [detail]

Flora MacDonald was arrested a few days after she helped the prince escape to Skye.

Allan Ramsay (1713–84), 1749, oil on canvas, 95 x 82.5 cm (framed), The Ashmolean Museum, Oxford. Bequeathed by the Revd Dr Richard Rawlinson, 1755, WA1960.76

Kings over the water

It was almost sixty years since Prince Charles Edward Stuart's grandfather, James VII & II, had lost his throne. With each passing decade the power of the exiled Stuarts, and ultimately their claim to the throne of the three kingdoms, diminished.

Those months as a fugitive had done little to deter Prince Charles and his quest for the British throne. Despite his defeat at Culloden he was given a hero's welcome on his return to France, receiving a standing ovation at the opera in Paris. Louis XV was at first gracious toward the prince, but his patience soon wore thin. Charles demanded that the king make resources immediately available for him to return to Scotland, but the French king had no intention of funding another venture.

Charles's father was by now resigned to never being restored and took solace in his faith. Henry similarly chose a life of dedication to the Catholic Church, despite the growing resentment of his brother. In April 1747 Henry, who was also in France, left Paris for Rome without telling Charles. A few days later James wrote to his eldest son, 'I know not whether you will be surprised, my dearest Carluccio [Charles], when I tell you that your brother will be made a Cardinal the first days of next month'. Unaware that his father had been encouraging Henry towards this new vocation, Charles described the news 'like a dagger to [his] heart'.

Although made a cardinal deacon in July 1747, Prince Henry was not yet ordained as a priest. This took place in September 1748. A few days later he celebrated his first Mass in the chapel royal, in front of his father and the Stuart court. Henry Benedict, Cardinal York, was now a Prince of the Catholic Church.

Charles knew that Henry's choice to become a cardinal would jeopardise his own chances of becoming ruler of the largely Protestant Britain. Bitterly disappointed by what he saw as betrayal by his family, he continued to pursue his claim to the British throne alone.

Opposite: Portrait of Prince Henry Benedict Clement Stuart (1725–1807) [detail]

Prince Henry is shown here in armour and wearing the Order of the Garter. Henry and Charles both sat for de la Tour between 1746–47, just before Henry was made a cardinal in the Catholic Church.

By Maurice Quentin de la Tour (1704–88), 1746–47, oil on canvas, Scottish National Portrait Gallery, Edinburgh, PG 2954

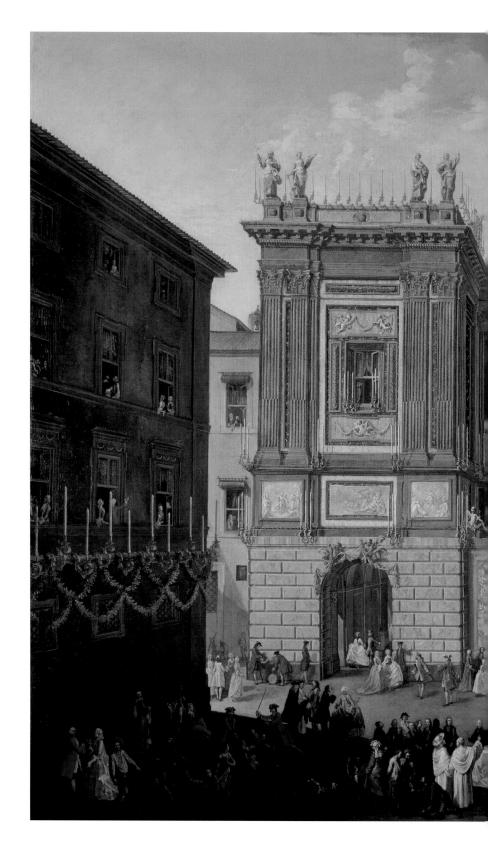

The Palazzo del Re, Rome [detail]

James VIII & III is shown here receiving his son, Prince Henry Benedict, in front of the Palazzo del Re, home to the exiled Jacobite court in Rome. They are celebrating Henry's appointment as cardinal deacon on 3 July 1747. James is greeting his younger son, who is dressed in the black coat, scarlet stockings and shoes with red heels often worn by cardinals in the 18th century. The palace has been lavishly 'dressed' with temporary architectural decoration, like a theatre set.

Paolo Monaldi (1720–99), Pubalacci and [Louis de?] Silvestri, c.1747/48, oil on canvas, Scottish National Portrait Gallery, Edinburgh, PG 3269

Left: Charlotte Stuart, Duchess of Albany (1753–89), daughter of Prince Charles Edward Stuart [detail]

Hugh Douglas Hamilton (c.1739–1808), 1785–86, oil on canvas, Scottish National Portrait Gallery, Edinburgh, PG 623

Right: Prince Charles Edward Stuart (1720–1788) [detail]

Hugh Douglas Hamilton (c.1739–1808), c.1785, oil on canvas, Scottish National Portrait Gallery, Edinburgh, PG 622

Opposite: Clementina Walkinshaw (c.1720–1802), mistress of Prince Charles Edward Stuart [detail]

Artist unknown, 1740–45, oil on canvas, Scottish National Portrait Gallery, Edinburgh, PG 1102

In 1748, the Treaty of Aix-la-Chapelle gave recognition to the Hanoverian succession in Britain and Charles was ordered out of France. Refusing to leave, Louis XV had him arrested and only released if he left the country immediately. For Charles there would be no more support from France. And worse, it seemed his own father had favoured Henry over him.

Charles led a nomadic existence for the next 17 years, his life now on a downward spiral. He engaged upon a series of affairs and drank to excess, although when required he was able to remain sober for long periods.

In 1750 Charles made a secret trip to London, where it was thought he converted to Anglicanism to make his claim to the British throne more acceptable. Two years later he encountered an old acquaintance, Clementina Walkinshaw, whom he first met in Scotland during the 1745 rising. She became his mistress and then mother of his daughter Charlotte, born on 23 October 1753. By 1760 Charles's erratic behaviour, often fuelled by alcohol, descended into physical violence towards Clementina. She left him, taking Charlotte, and for over twelve years they lived estranged from Charles in different convents in France.

Charles married Louise of Stolberg, a German princess, in 1772. It was a childless marriage and Louise, like Clementina, left him because of his abusive behaviour.

Charlotte and her father were eventually reconciled. In 1784 he recognised her as his heir and bestowed the Scottish title of Duchess of Albany upon her. Charlotte cared for Charles until his death in 1788.

Death of the king

James VIII & III died on 1 January 1766 at the Palazzo del Re in Rome. Charles had been told that his father was dying, but he arrived in the city three weeks too late. Father and son had not seen each other in person since 1744, although they had corresponded more regularly just before James's death.

With no support from France or Spain, Charles needed the Pope, at that time Clement XIII, to recognise him as the rightful king of Britain on the death of his father. Henry pleaded with the Pope to declare his brother Charles III, but to no avail. In 1766 Clement acknowledged the House of Hanover as the rightful rulers of Britain and Ireland.

James was buried in St Peter's Basilica in 1766, the only king to have been accorded this right. When Charles died in 1788 he was buried in the Cathedral Basilica of St Peter Apostle in Frascati. At Henry's death in 1807, both brothers were laid to rest beside their father on 16 July of that year. Three simple marble plaques marked their resting place.

A monument to the Jacobite Stuart kings, designed by Antonio Canova, was commissioned by Monsignor Cesarini, executor of Henry Benedict's estate. Opposite the monument is one that is dedicated to Queen Maria Clementina, commissioned by Pope Benedict XIV and sculpted by Pietro Bracci.

In 1938 the bodies of the three kings were moved to a new site in the crypt of St Peter's Basilica. Because of the close association between the Stuart dynasty and Scotland, the grave markers were transferred to the Pontifical Scots College, Rome, in 1939.

The College was established in 1600 as a school for Scottish Catholic men. Since 1616 it has been a seminary for those training for the priesthood from the Catholic dioceses of Scotland. In 1964 the College moved from central Rome to a new site and the grave markers were installed in the College chapel.

Opposite: Engraving of the funeral procession of James VIII & III, 1766 [detail]

1766, paper, Scottish National Portrait Gallery, Edinburgh, SP EXL 59 1

...latio Corporis ...Britanniae Franciae, et Hiberniae Regis, in qua ...ibi justa a CLEMENTE XIII. P. M. ...silicam Vaticanam, ubi situm est, ...II. Idus Januarias, anno MDCCLXVI.

HONI SOIT QUI MAL Y PENSE

DIEU ET MON DROIT

...like me... ...conglobes in my eye...

...isdeem... ...diffical...

...nde der may... ...in a sigh,

...at li...

...me...

...de... ...throne;

...degenerate son...

...offeringly slight it...

...obliged humble serv.
...Burns

Symbols of support

Opposite: Wine glass and letter

This letter was written by Robert Burns in 1787, accepting an invitation to dine on the anniversary of the prince's birthday. The glass, one of six, was commissioned by Thomas Erskine, later 9th Earl of Kellie.

Letter, 1787; wine glass, *c*.1775, National Museums Scotland, H.OP 7 and H.MEN 94

Page 70: Wine glass, engraved with Jacobite emblems

c.1745–50, English, National Museums Scotland, A.1936.209

Page 71: Selection of wine glasses

Left and right are examples of Jacobite 'Amen' glasses, engraved with a crown above 'JR' and '8' for James VIII & III.

National Museums Scotland, A.1952.71, H.MEN 94 and 92

Wine glasses were an essential part of the secret ceremonies of Jacobite clubs and societies. Here groups of trusted friends declared their loyalty to the exiled Stuart dynasty by toasting the 'King over the Water'. A glass of wine would be held above a bowl of water, representing the sea separating Jacobites from their exiled king. In the early 18th century, drinking the health of the 'Pretender' was considered a serious offence, punishable by fine or even imprisonment.

The glasses were engraved with coded emblems and mottos, often in Latin, as veiled demonstrations of loyalty to the Stuarts. Many of these expressed hope for a swift restoration of the exiled dynasty.

Popular mottos included *Radiat*, 'It shines'; *Radeat*, 'May he return'; *Rede*, 'Return'; and *Reditti*, 'Restore'.

Other common motifs were the white rose, which symbolised James VIII & III, and rosebuds representing the two princes – an open larger bud for Charles Edward and a closed bud for Henry Benedict.

Jacobite symbols and mottos also featured on fans, jewellery and snuff boxes. These were personal objects that were only to be shared with like-minded friends.

70

Royal relations

The beginnings of reconciliation between the exiled Stuarts and the ruling Hanoverians occurred at the end of the 18th century during the reign of George III. The Jacobite kings and their supporters were no longer seen as a threat to the British monarchy. Charles Edward had died in 1788 and Henry Benedict, Cardinal York, despite being acknowledged as Henry IX by his Jacobite followers, had made no claim on the throne.

In the aftermath of the French Revolution, Henry lost the income from his properties in France. He also lost his Italian home in Frascati. When George III was alerted to Henry's financial circumstances he provided him with a pension. Henry, however, considered this as long overdue compensation: despite the promises of successive British governments, the dowry of his grandmother, Mary of Modena, had never been paid to the Stuarts in exile.

It was the next king, George IV, who purchased the Stuart papers for the royal archives. He and his brother, the Duke of Sussex, were fascinated by Jacobitism, wearing Highland dress as early as 1789.

In part due to her love of the Highlands, Queen Victoria also felt an affinity with the exiled dynasty, declaring:

I feel a sort of reverence in going over these scenes in this most beautiful country, which I am proud to call my own, where there was such devoted loyalty to the family of my ancestors – for Stuart blood is in my veins, and I am now their representative, and the people are as devoted and loyal to me as they were to that unhappy race.

From the House of Hanover to the present House of Windsor, works of fine and decorative art associated with the exiled Stuarts have been acquired for the Royal Collections, such as the broth bowl and stand opposite.

Opposite: Broth bowl, cover and stand

Probably owned by Prince Charles Edward, this broth bowl and stand shows the Stuart coat of arms and may have been commissioned by the prince when he lodged briefly at the château de Vincennes in 1748. The bowl and cover were purchased by Queen Elizabeth II.

French, *c.*1748, porcelain, The Royal Collection / HM Queen Elizabeth II 2017, RCIN 19605 a–c

Acknowledgements

Opposite: Prince Charles Edward Stuart (1720–88)

By Louis Gabriel Blanchet (1705–72), *c.*1739, oil on canvas, The Royal Collection / HM Queen Elizabeth II 2017, RCIN 401208

Page 78: Broadsword

Hilt made by Charles Frederick Kandler, *c.*1738–41, steel blade with gilded decoration, solid silver hilt, 95 cm (length), National Museums Scotland, H.MCR 2

Page 79: Scroll-butt pistols, owned by the Earls of Stair [details] (see page 18)

By Alexander Logan or Adam Lawson, *c.*1660, Scottish, 66 cm (length), National Museums Scotland, H.LH 433 and 434

Page 80: Tartan suit of Sir John Hynde Cotton of Madingley, Cambridgeshire [detail]

*c.*1744, Scottish, wool and silk, National Museums Scotland, K.2005.16.1 to 3

National Museums Scotland would like to thank the following sources for images and objects used in this book, and assistance with its publication:

© Ashmolean Museum, University of Oxford – page 58; National Galleries of Scotland / Scottish National Portrait Gallery, Edinburgh – pages 17 (right), 31, 48 (left), 61, 62–63, 64 (all), 65, 67; Reproduced by permission of the National Library of Scotland – page 29; © National Maritime Museum Greenwich, London – pages 40–41; © National Museums Scotland – pages 1, 2–3, 8, 9 (left), 12, 16, 17 (left), 18 (all), 19, 24–25, 26, 27, 28 (all), 29 (right), 30 (all), 35, 36 (all), 38, 39 (all), 42 (all), 43, 44 (all), 45, 46, 47, 48 (right), 49, 50, 51, 54, 55 (all), 56 (all), 59 (all), 68, 70, 71, 78, 79, 80; © National Portrait Gallery, London – page 15; With grateful thanks to the Pininski Foundation, Warsaw, Poland – page 34; Prussian Palaces and Garden Foundation Berlin – Brandenberg / Photographer Wolfgang Pfauder – page 21; Royal Collection Trust / © Her Majesty Queen Elizabeth II 2017 – pages 6, 9 (right), 11, 22–23, 37, 52–53, 73, 74; The Royal College of Physicians of Edinburgh – page 57; © UK Government Art Collection – page 32.

Acquired with the aid of the Heritage Lottery Fund and the Art Fund – page 9 (left); Lent by the Scottish Roman Catholic Hierarchy. Lent by the Congregation of the Ursulines of Jesus – page 12; Acquired with the aid of the National Heritage Memorial Fund – page 26; Acquired with the aid of the Art Fund – pages 8, 35, 36 (left). (All images © National Museums Scotland).

Art Fund_

With grateful thanks to the curators, conservators, photographers, picture library and publishing staff, collections services, exhibition, design and administrative staff who have contributed to this book. And our gratitude to Edward Corp for advice and assistance with the exhibition and publications.

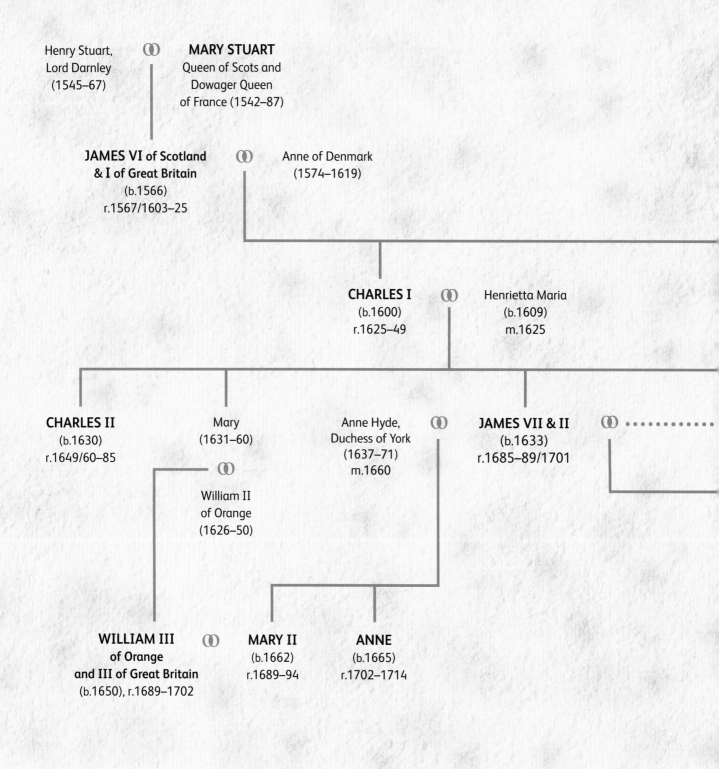

Henry Stuart,
Lord Darnley
(1545–67)

⊕

MARY STUART
Queen of Scots and
Dowager Queen
of France (1542–87)

**JAMES VI of Scotland
& I of Great Britain**
(b.1566)
r.1567/1603–25

⊕

Anne of Denmark
(1574–1619)

CHARLES I
(b.1600)
r.1625–49

⊕

Henrietta Maria
(b.1609)
m.1625

CHARLES II
(b.1630)
r.1649/60–85

Mary
(1631–60)

Anne Hyde,
Duchess of York
(1637–71)
m.1660

⊕

JAMES VII & II
(b.1633)
r.1685–89/1701

⊕ ••••••••••••

⊕

William II
of Orange
(1626–50)

WILLIAM III
of Orange
and III of Great Britain
(b.1650), r.1689–1702

⊕

MARY II
(b.1662)
r.1689–94

ANNE
(b.1665)
r.1702–1714

The Stuart dynasty family tree

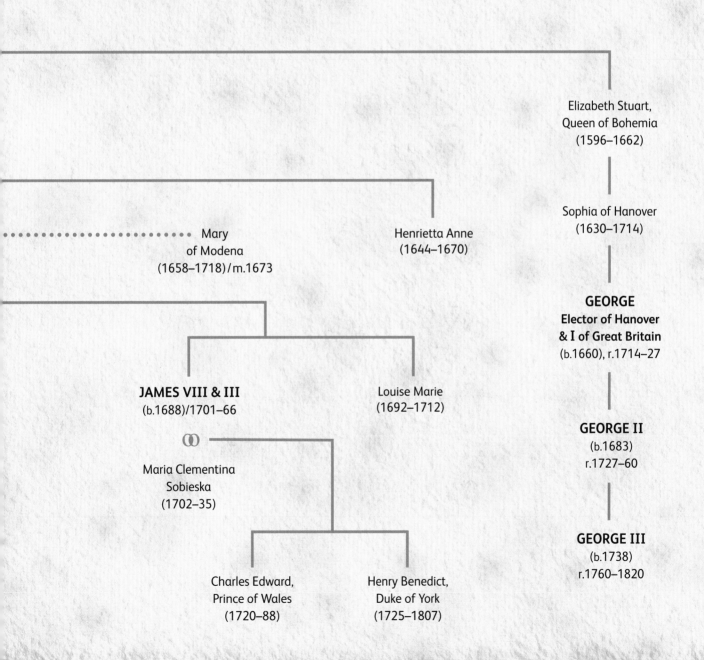

Elizabeth Stuart,
Queen of Bohemia
(1596–1662)

Sophia of Hanover
(1630–1714)

GEORGE
Elector of Hanover
& I of Great Britain
(b.1660), r.1714–27

GEORGE II
(b.1683)
r.1727–60

GEORGE III
(b.1738)
r.1760–1820

Mary
of Modena
(1658–1718)/m.1673

Henrietta Anne
(1644–1670)

JAMES VIII & III
(b.1688)/1701–66

Louise Marie
(1692–1712)

Maria Clementina
Sobieska
(1702–35)

Charles Edward,
Prince of Wales
(1720–88)

Henry Benedict,
Duke of York
(1725–1807)

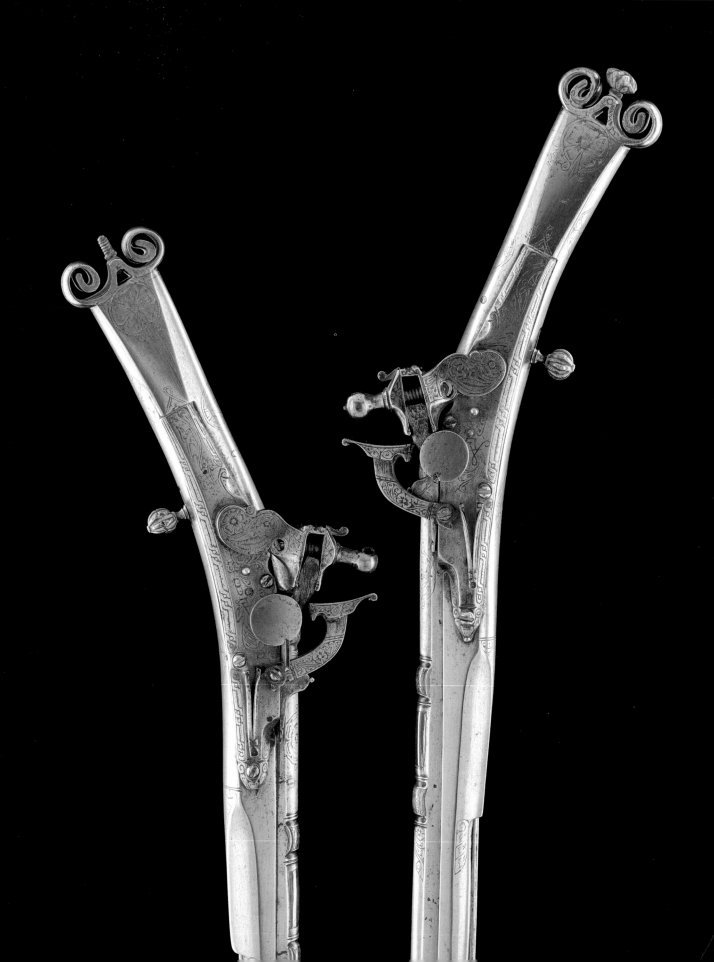